If I Were Blind

Feral Poetry · Volume 1
B. Charles Dorsey

ISBN: 978-0-692-69492-3

Copyright 2016 by B. Charles Dorsey

Book Design by David Freeman
Freeman Design

Feral Poetry

Feral (adj.). < *L. fera, wild animal* < *ferus, fierce*.
1. Untamed; wild. 2. Savage. 3. Having reverted to the wild state, as from domestication.

Traditional poetry, like the pig, is a domesticated beast. It can be managed, categorized, kept in a pen, and fed on table scraps. It tastes like bacon. Feral poetry, on the other hand, is wild, like a peccary. It roams free. It can't be trained, and it won't come when it's called. It will raid your trash can, dig up your garden, chase your children and small dogs.

These are feral poems. They are short, they take lots of line breaks, and sometimes they even rhyme. But just because they look like poetry doesn't mean they are poetry. Their behaviors—the ways they go a' wandering—are unexpected and unpredictable. They don't follow conventions or rules. To appreciate them, you must follow them home, to where they live, out there in the wilderness.

CONTENTS

LOVE

Past Tense 1
The Hand that Fits in Mine 3
At a Glance 4
Morning Song 5
If I Were Blind 6
Like Acknowledged Humiliation 7
Moments of Perfect Convergence 8
More Lovely in His Mind 9
The Accounts of a Young Man's Heart 10
The River Bend 12
Theoretical Mathematics 13
Your Hands 15
You Don't Remember 16
Always 18

LIFE

Living on the Bias 21
All the Marbles 23
Another Gravity Junky 24
Deaf to Damn Near 25
East Wind 27
My Truck Awaits at the Bottom of the Road . . . 29

Really Gone 32
When I Was a Child. 34
The Ungloved Hand. 35
Polygamy 36
Valuables 37
So Go the Groceries 38
If You Ride a White Horse 39

WISDOM
A Bit of Shit Upon My Shoe 43
What Feels Good in the Hand 45
Wrong Way Buffet 46
Regarding Emily Dickinson 47
The Village Idiot. 48
My Mother's Words 50
Different and the Same. 51
Clean the Glass 53
We Begin Early. 54
Spring Just Went Past. 55
Personification 56
Street Lady. 57
Life Ain't Made for Lookin' 58
Empty Buckets. 59
Building a Rock Wall 60
For Just 60 Seconds 62

THE DARK CLOSET

Freedom from the Need to Know. 65

Gamblers 66

How God Screwed Up 67

Now That I Am Dead. 69

Fender Skirt 70

Whackin' the Sack 71

Worry. 72

I Can't Not Love This World 73

LOVE

PAST TENSE

He's driven his high profile
relationship vehicle off the road
so many times he's legend
in ditches around here.

Rather than fail to negotiate
another straight-a-way, he's decided
to leave that 'feels so-fine-to-slide-inside,
quick-acceleration, high-RPM,
can't-keep-this-shiny-assed-rig-on-the-road'
right where he last lost
control of it and wait.

And he did, for a while, watching
other sweet-running relationships
purr past, taking notice that
most were contented sedans,
maintaining a modest velocity.
And he began to entertain
the possibility
of getting back on the road.
As all urges breed action,
verbs become past tense.
So before you know it he's back in
another vehicle, a used model to be sure,
but you could tell by her shine
and lines that there was a
go fast under the skirt.

He did miss much about it:
the purr in his ear, the tingle of controlling
where she went and how fast she got there,
the feel of her classic curves under his hand,
the warmth from her engine rising up to him.

You could see his body thrum
with anticipation each time he'd
ease into her, caressing the sweet carnal
circle of the steering wheel, resting his hand
on the kinetic energy vibrating off that
gear shift knob sticking straight
up through the floor.

Drive-drove
see-saw
do-did
fling-flang
and that newest relationship vehicle
is wrecked, right there in the ditch
where Aphrodite
flang it.

THE HAND THAT FITS IN MINE

We learn early the comfort that
comes with holding hands.

Big hands first, guiding and
supporting, loving hands,

a mother's hand that completes
our partial self. We learn that mother's

hand like our own. Like the
womb, it folds around our helplessness.

There are other hands: rough hands,
soft hands, sister hands, brother hands.

As our hands grow more able, we begin
to imagine ourselves independent,

not needing another's hand. Then, like
autumn changes the sky of summer,

our heart says 'now,' and our hands begin
their cardinal search for a companion,

somewhere out there a hand that
fits perfectly in ours, and we learn

that hand, like our own, as it folds
around us the rest of our lives.

AT A GLANCE

Snuggling between the clinic and the medical lab
like the cleavage of another chance, sat the convenience store
which he entered hungry, road-soaked, unloved.

The double take he offers the young woman
in the black dress is a reflection, a knee jerk
he can't even consciously control.

She, an off-duty lab technician working next door,
received his interest as a compliment, but
knew men's eye were only capable of summary focus. He had
seen her hair or her breasts, so needed a second opinion.
She wondered if he knew the urine samples sat
in the lab, sharing a wall with the beer cooler.

She had in fact given him a thorough check-up as they passed
between the bread and cereal, a woman's fleeting regard,
an affecting of innocence so subtle he didn't know that he had been
seized, stripped, prodded, that she'd drawn his blood,
that at a glance a woman will conduct a comprehensive examination
and with a high degree of probability
find her subject unfit.

If he should merit a double take, it will be so precise
he won't know the procedure has been performed,
like he is under anesthesia over there,
squeezing the buns on the top shelf.

MORNING SONG

It's going to be a good day,
my shadow, sitting on the
west wall, is telling me
as I write at the kitchen table.

The old wood stove is popping through
its warm works, keeping us companion
along with these quiet words
I write for you.

Asleep in the bedroom, your hair flares
across the pillow, rewarding
my eyes with your slender neck.
I ease into bed, pull close,

purse my lips to be ever so lightly
drawn along that treasure route
of fine hair, down across the topography
of your shoulder, plunging like a renegade

into the sweet grass hollow of your back.
But words are backing up, my shadow is waiting,
and above the ticking of the cooling stove,
I hear your husband's car approaching.

IF I WERE BLIND

If I were blind
I could locate the sun
allow its warmth to fall upon my cheek

If I were blind
I could turn my ear to the wren
let its melody draw my smile

If I were blind
I could lift my face to the pine tree
have its dark green scent explain the softness beneath my feet

If I were blind
I could still taste the sensual sweetness of a peach
and summer would pass into me

If I were blind
I could fall on my back into the snow
feel the earth hold me like a mother

If I were blind
I could run my fingers over the soft corners of your shoulder
and recognize the center of my universe

But the baby I saw in the store today was blind
will grow up in a world meant for eyes
never knowing love at first sight or blue.
It is prophetic bullshit for me to imagine if I were blind.
When I close my eyes there is only darkness.

LIKE ACKNOWLEDGED HUMILIATION

Roxy Benjamin was
my sister's friend, eleven maybe,
living at the end of our road.

I taught her how to ride my bike,
she taught me how to whistle.

She lost control, rode into a ditch
and sprained her wrist.

With her other hand she
touched my lips to form
that first whistle.

A sensation gushed through my body
like acknowledged humiliation.

At nine I learned
that I loved women.

And listen.
I can whistle.

MOMENTS OF PERFECT CONVERGENCE

Rare moments of perfect convergence
Not how we'd have our inspiration spread
That would be evenly across the continuum
Like warm butter on homemade bread

But moments of perfect convergence
Come unexpected like love, lust, and fate
When we're too implicated in our enchantment
To hear implausibility's horse at the gate

Like a crossing of paths in the morning
Of sunshine and what you desire
With a measure of lust for adventure
In presence of encouragement's choir

The collision of light, sound, and color
In absence of time's common sense
When health dances with good intention
And you're indifferent to risk's consequence

Or when your lover's mind is uncluttered
She invites you into her robe
And you're lost in a whirl of arousal
A convocation that never grows old

Rare moments of perfect convergence
Not how we'd have our inspiration spread
That would be evenly across the continuum
Like warm butter on homemade bread

But moments of perfect convergence
Come unexpected like love, lust, and fate
When we're too implicated in our enchantment
To hear impossibility's horse at the gate

MORE LOVELY IN HIS MIND

After all those years of living with her
Harbored within the grace of her acumen
And goodness
That informal radiance
Seeing her inadvertently beautiful
And consciously stunning
She had become even more lovely
To him in his mind than in his eye
So during short periods of separation
His desire for her boiled
And reunions were torrid
Perilous to the heart of an old man,
the passionate hero of his own novel.

THE ACCOUNTS OF A YOUNG MAN'S HEART

A sweet pungency of second-cut hay
suspends the long August twilight
like a spoiled summer child
refusing to surrender to sleep

A cadence of metered hay bales
line up, obedient soldiers, cross
a broad undulating parade ground

Swallow and nighthawks swim
across a sky so thick with summer
we can't hope to identify a simple flavor

Now the evening cool sinks beneath
the sweltering seam of dust and color
to paint a fresh coat across the hayfield
and grandmothers emerge to sit on porches

Pickup trucks interrupt the tick of crickets
trailing swells of dust to deliver friends,
smelling of soap and hair cream,
to a promised harvest hayride

The rattle of the tractor blends with
the pandemonium of frogs as we're towed
around the pond, all tucked in crannies
between bales on the hay wagon

In the clutches of a classmate named Sally,
affirming the suspicions of a girl fifteen
that they hold proxy for the
accounts of young men's hearts

And me, a specimen of innocence
swept along in the exhilaration of her wake
my hands accepting her invitations tentatively
on the frontier of an untested libido

All flavor I can taste now
only as reconstituted yearning.
Magic moments precede knowing
as we are passengers in a vehicle with no reverse
only a rear-view mirror

THE RIVER BEND

We came upon the cabin,
silent and dark, sitting right
on the river. We had taken
an oxbow shortcut that
had us lost and walking in a
wrong direction, away from the day.
It grew darker with every step.
We both masked our worry,
but we were in a fix.

The cabin door, unlocked, an
'Enjoy and be kind' sign in the window,
invited us in. Wood was already on the grate.
The fire filled our bonanza cabin with warm shadows.

We shared the big soft chair
pulled up to the fireplace, roasted
the Vienna sausages we found
in the cupboard, and watched steam
tickle off our wet socks.

The river held us in the palm of its drone,
above the owl and coyote's night.
We told family stories and made love
on the squeaky bed in the corner
where we woke at dawn to the
nuthatch and the towhee.

You made coffee while I
stoked the fire, and we
gave ourselves up for lost.

THEORETICAL MATHEMATICS

I dated a young theoretical mathematician
For a short while, she had a perfect
L X H X W = 6.1
Golden ratio body

I have yet to discover what the formula
Was that attracted her to me, but I'm
Certain she saw me as a problem
She could solve

I was, after all, linear and stable
She once told me after sex that
I was a marble in a bowl, predictably
Returning to sit quietly at the bottom
Mathematicians love linear and stable,
At least for a while, then by accretion
They develop a need for challenge
A little unpredictability: chaos

Maybe that is not just mathematicians,
Maybe that is women. My chaos came
With alcohol and dancing in a wild
And socially arrhythmic flailing manner

That she said even embarrassed people
Who weren't dancing with me. This
Was the perturbation, deviance she
Called it, that drew the system out of

Solvable balance and kept her in the
System a few months longer than I
Expected her to stay. Then one morning
After sex again she announced,

Given I now understand your starting coordinates
And parameters with the simple equation
X (my future) = rx (1-x) I can see where you are
headed and I don't want to be part of the system
when you get there.

YOUR HANDS

The conference table was crowded
and I lost interest in the meeting
early. Left my eyes to wandering.
They found your hands.

Four or five down from me,
only your hands,
small, olive-toned, and polite.
I paused to wonder who
they belonged to, but
could not follow them up to you.

Circling the table my eyes passed over
faces attentive and uninteresting,
and other hands, painted and ringed.
Then returned to your hands, I named them:

Young and Defined. And again they
ransomed my imagination.
I studied these servants of your ideas,
strong and growing restless.
Watched them play with the pencil,
Catholic hands, adventurous,
But not impetuous.

I became your illicit lover
With having only seen your hands
Those puppets of your soul.

YOU DON'T REMEMBER

Remember those autumn hikes,
hand in hand, the ones you said
you'd never forget…that you forgot?

The trail carpeted in leaves, memorable
in gaudy palette of red, gold, and green
that painted your path with infatuation.

And the smell; fertility that comes with death,
the earth opening her legs to the fall rains
after the parch of summer. The woods
nearly naked, allowing the last bars of sunlight
to penetrate.

Under the equinox drifts, tree roots
hidden, reach out playfully to catch your feet
and there, listen…

You hear the breeze before you see it,
like a train, it hurried to nudge the leaves,
just deciding. We waited, embracing,
for them to dance out of the sky,
the first snowflakes of winter landing
like geese, feet forward, on the stream,
to be carried on the determined,
downward journey to the sea.

As you shivered out of the chilly shadows
cast by wisps of horsetail clouds sneaking in,
to cross the guaranteed sky, portents of change.
Your feet chased up mingled leaves,
whis, whis, like frightened cats,
they scattered aside.

You don't remember, do you?
The vivid impression on your senses diminished
like magnetism with distance, like the faded
scarlet maple leaf you pressed between
the pages of promises you carefully wrote
in your diary that autumn to
love me, always.
You don't remember
You don't remember

ALWAYS

Always is not 50.

Always is that you're a perfect mother,
love always unconditional, self-sacrifice
always on the table.

Always is that you're a good friend,
loyal, supportive, always there.

Always is that you are a beauty
outside and in. For those who know you
that beauty is like a default, absolute.
For those who don't, that beauty
always turns heads.

Always is your trust, optimism, and goodness,
and always your common sense, humor, and humility.

Always is how long I want you to be my wife
because always you are my source of calm
and model of moderation, my counselor,
my friend, my fan club president,
my social counterbalance, my idol,
my lover, my life.

Always you make me proud and complete my circle.
Always is how long I will love you.

Always is not 50, but
you are.

LIFE

LIVING ON THE BIAS

On the bias, ask
any seamstress to explain,
is sewing at a diagonal
to the fabric's natural grain.

Like ferrying across a current
not rowing with the stream
is different than expected
and easier than it seems.

When you live on the bias
many are those who will ask
"Isn't your direction misdirected
to gratify society's task?"

That trend, of course, of culture,
safe behavior for a sheep,
the debt, the car, the trophy house
with palatial lawns to keep.

But life upon the bias
cuts across this busy road,
not decision by appearance,
it's experience that is gold.

It's choosing to live blue collar,
to sweat and work by hand,
dedication to worthy causes
benefiting earth and man.

It's separating ranks by age group
gated communities and large RV's,
ignoring polls and markets
and provincial tendencies

Boycotting air conditioning
and convenient gadgetry
saving rivers for the salmon
not more electricity

It's stooping for a penny
disregarded for lack of worth,
collecting cans and bottles
for the deposit and the earth.

To live days with singularity
not bound by what's required
like eating Vienna sausages
with a borrowed pair of pliers.

ALL THE MARBLES

Clearies, cat's eyes, swirls, they came
fast and erratic. On my knees
in the dirt I scooped them up
stuffing my pockets with greedy hands.

A stooped vulture, my smile
reflected back at me, contorted like
gluttony off the shiny silver-dollar-sized
steely resting seductively in the shallow pit.

From twenty-five paces covetous fifth grade boys
rolled impossible prayers across the hard pan
playground toward the pot holding the prize,
credulous children at a carnival game.

A gift from my mechanic father,
the heavy ball bearing encumbered one pocket,
the marbles of victory counterbalanced in the other,
I led the glum parade of defeated warriors in from
recess.

My pants hanging contingent on my skinny ass,
I was intercepted at the schoolhouse door,
escorted to the dreaded office of confessions,
forced to surrender my profits.

The game of potsies prohibited, the
notion of supply and demand repealed,
the perpetrator's mother called.

ANOTHER GRAVITY JUNKY

All you downstream water,
who is your master?
Who is insisting you descend
so tenaciously, never sleeping,

forcing yourself along channels too small
for you to comfortably pass?
The becoming agitated,
froth and roar, getting so worked up
it is miles before you are calm again,
this fidelity so unusual with soldiers.
Is it the promise of return
that draws you so relentlessly,
your ocean yearning?

Possibly it's an accumulation of responsibility,
taking on the identities of tributaries
under your name that inspires you to
push unremitting, with this
abiding persistence.
There's something,
something invisible
compelling you to this
exertion through canyons.

Could it be
you're just another
gravity junky?

Riding the welfare cabby,
on the cheap,
in the one direction that offers
free immediate gratification?

Down.

DEAF TO DAMN NEAR

If he had an ear for anything
it certainly wouldn't be whether
his guitar was in tune
or if he was singing in key.

If he had an ear for anything
it would be rhyme, get him started
and you'd think him descendent of
Alexander Pope; this is important-

A life of disregard for the future
he doubted would come, of ears unprotected, of
chainsaws, gunfire, and oversized amps,
left him with hearing loss within
the human voice range the size of a siren sky,
a flat spot in his audiogram like
someone pulled the plug.

A vanity only slightly smaller denied him
the use of hearing devices,
so he was compelled to compensate during conversations
where three out of five words sounded like a
road map being folded in a wind storm

Words like nice sounded like rice
and he'd be chatting chicken recipes
during a discussion about the weather,
but thanks to rhyme he could fill in
those blanks without hesitation, never
intentionally obtuse or purposefully rude,
living in a context auditorially skewed.

His conversation was lively; he was deaf not mute,
a perky plus-sixty man the young women thought cute
which is the first signal, chronological weather vane
that, like a grandfather, he was growing inane.

So as not to allow
this advantage to pass,
when she asked for his help
with finding the path
he obliged by placing
his hand on her ass.

EAST WIND

It whispered its intent
to the morning grass.
We did not notice until
it had spread through the day
and usurped the afternoon.
It came headlong from a

direction we did not expect,
and the leaves, wearing their
late September shirts of ochre and cerise,
anticipating the daily westerly,
were so startled they let go
to dance through the charged air,
a million twirls.

Frantic dogs ran nostrils flared,
cats hunkered under porches,
birds left unwelcome perches
to swerve and soar.

This wind was solicitous, and
we yearned to turn our backs to it,
to move away from familiar places
to see the other side of those
we'd been following.

We held our heads differently
in this allegorical air,
attended to glints appearing
out of the corner of our eyes,
anticipating something unexpected.

We moved into inviolable wind shadows
places to relax our shoulders
to briefly rest ourselves where
the sun's warm could accumulate undistressed.
We watched out at the dust and leaves
in a high state of excitement
and were coerced to reenter
this game of chase, to feel
the disobedience of its incongruity.

The moon came to settle
this silly Chinook wind, to bring
peace to the disturbance of the day.
And we combed our hair
from an uncommon part, and understood
we can have our sovereign flags, but
it's up to the wind
which way they wave.

MY TRUCK AWAITS AT THE BOTTOM OF THE ROAD

For several weeks each winter
the temperamental jet stream
tilts in off the Pacific, like a Jezebel,
across our mountains to indulge herself
in carnal liaison with
some burly Canadian cold front.

The earth pulls a blanket of snow
over its head so as not to witness,
the trees lower their faces in contempt,
and the sun looks away.

During this interlude of intemperance
where the world blushes without color,
my old red truck waits for me
at the bottom of the road.

As the morning skulks in from the night, unpronounced,
its partnership with the sky cloaked in unaccustomed confidentiality,
I set off down the road
disguised by rubber and wool.

The quiet is deep;
only the cadence of my steps on crisp untried snow
accompanies me.
My shadow is unemployed in the
pall of this crepuscular light.

Cloven indentions show the deer have
preceded me into the day,
watching now, demure, behind the heavy skirts
of weeping boughs
like children of paradise.

Emboldened by the cold stillness
my timid breath presents itself
and trails off behind me
like the taste of an orange.

In the white filigree of branches above
A dark flittering named
Nuthatch, Junco, Chickadee
disturbs the new snow.

As with all downward routes, mine ultimately
bring me to a creek.
Whispering its intent to drain this place,
it carves a dark animation across the
rich man's robe of white inertness.

Upstream a single rock, unexpected,
reaching out of the water,
vibrant, green with moss,
hooks my eye as easily as
capturing a summer memory.

I am detained in this moment
of perfect convergence,
and I wonder: if man stands still enough,
with commensurate respect in his solitude,
might he regain the understanding
of what it means to be part of this natural world,
not an enemy to it?

A jay, intruding from above,
Calls, 'Now,'
and I raise my eyes into the alders
to address some unstated intensity,
the day growing stronger,
and I realize I've lingered too long.

I pick up my bag, askew in the snow,
and move away from this
harmony of will and intellect
that I've bartered for money.

Most of a mile from my house
I come to my truck,
waiting, passive and unfailing,
where the snowplow has
rediscovered the road.

REALLY GONE

Is my dog really gone, now
I've buried her in the ground
A story with THE END, a
Bird song with the sound?

Is a relationship really over
With the finality of goodbye
Unremembered bitterness
Your parents when they die?

When the fire burns the log
Is it really gone? An apple
When it's eaten,
The lyrics with the song?

Is your shadow really gone
When you walk into the shade
Can you name yourself successful
For the money that you've made?

Are nightmares gone with morning
And daydreams with the night?
Is summer gone with autumn
Or anger with our spite?

Is your work really done
When you come in from the barn?
Are you in the arms of safety
When out of the reach of harm?

Is anything really gone,
A day, a dream, a thought?
Feeling for a lover,
Hurt that you have wrought?

Are classes really over
With the ringing of the bell? Or
Just a dusting off of hands on
The progressive path to hell?

WHEN I WAS A CHILD

Before church got a hold of me
and I was forced to study science,
I held a manageable grip on reality.

We had a finite amount of hair rolled up
on spindles beneath our follicles that would
run out with too many haircuts. It already had on
Gordon's head; he was my momma's boy friend.

My pee was yellow from playing in the sun,
and when I drank hot chocolate or milk, the
brown went to my bad and the white to my good,
so as long as I drank lots of milk I was okay.

Everyone had a fire hose. Girls were different
only because they didn't like trucks. The
refrigerator was cold because the milk was
in there, and night was the day gone to bed.

My mother had eyes in the back of her head;
her hair was long so she could hide them. And
God was some old white guy watching me from
the clouds, so at night I was exempt from scrutiny.

People got smaller as they moved away from me
because I was already forgetting about them.
Things fell down because if they fell up they'd
Disappear, and you would never get them back.

Listen, I'm not telling you anything you don't
already know: lies were baby stomach aches,
'I'm sorry' were magic words to get you out of trouble,
and like your hair you had a limited amount of 'I'm sorry's,
but whenever your mother called you by your full name
you'd cash them in immediately.

THE UNGLOVED HAND

When, like an ambush, the sun
struck the meadow, the elk hurried
their hunger to the shadows and
the wan promise of safety.

A green frog, sitting motionless as
though giving birth to an idea, imagines
he's invisible to the snake who knows
without seeing what's for dinner.

There was in the meadow that was
her town an opposite aunt I never
met who gave the wood of her
future to the fire of her youth.

'Bold,' said uncle Orville.
'Beyond beautiful,' said her sister.
'Dangerous,' said her father.
'Magnetic,' said her sister's husband.
'Crazy.' This was her mother.

Unlike the elk, she stood in the sunlight.
Unlike the frog, she didn't blend in.
She moved alone; there was no competition;
but as always there were predators.

In her meadow, the wind leaped in like
an unpaid mortgage, a leaden mask
of clouds hid the stage light of sun
and sequined garment of her beauty

but couldn't keep her safe against
the snake, who knew without seeing
that the well fed were bold and
vulnerable, like an ungloved hand.

POLYGAMY

The belt I wore to work today is
The same belt I wore to work yesterday

The only belt I've worn since 1976
The only belt I have, like my wife

I wonder if polygamists have more
Than one belt, and if so, why?

One to hold up their pants, and the other,
Like a second wife, to hang themselves with?

VALUABLES

He brings it from his pocket
like something alive,
his fat little fingers struggling to perform
without guidance of his eyes,
the other hand holding up his pants.

They say a raccoon, once his fist is closed around
a treasure, won't relax
it even to escape. Just so our little presenter
must have help to extract
his fist from his pocket.

With all the adults bent low, and
his big sister on her knees,
her nose to his hand, his fingers
begin their release,
like the opening of a time-lapsed flower.

"Gravel!" an incredulous voice reports, and
we stand with condescending smirks on our faces.
His sister moves in closer, her pretty brown finger
touching one of the jagged places.
" Look!" she exclaims. "It's a diamond!"

He moves his hand out from under hers,
"No," he says. "It's a mountain. See here are the trees!"
We lean in for a second look, let our inspection
follow the slope of its windward and lee,
and give each other affirming nods.

There's a collective recognition in our bobbing heads
that the erosion of innocence has a cost,
of a precious wisdom that can't be gained but only lost.
Gold is only as valuable as we think it is.

SO GO THE GROCERIES

The prophet said, 'Believe
The light, it has no reason
To lie to you

As it lays across your arm
You notice the texture
Of your skin

Slackening, like ripple marks
On fine sand. Sun, water
Stress and sweat,

Chlorine pools, cold air out
Car windows and warm
Embraces coalescing,

Molecules of water at the tip
Of an ice cycle, growing into
A drop so heavy

It must fall, wrinkling
The surface of the pool below
Exposing the fragility

Of reflection.' The prophet said,
'Believe your eyes; they
Tell the truth.

The bag you came in is getting
Thin, and as goes the bag
So go the groceries within.'

IF YOU RIDE A WHITE HORSE

If you ride a white horse in your dreams
to visit another woman, the legend says,
you must never step down from that horse again.

And the other woman owns that horse,
and so it is when she calls her horse you are
drawn like low pressure pulls air from high.

And like that air you must adapt your existence
to belong to the weather on your planet:
sometimes still, holding the fragrance of hibiscus,

often mild with shadows when you think you see
where you are standing, but like the woman with
the white horse you are beckoned and can't resist.

Dark clouds fill your sky, and a great tumult sets
upon you, and you know you are your own fault.
The sincerity of captivity entangles you
and you'll desire to slip off that horse.
But as the parable teaches, what you mount
you must ride.

WISDOM

A BIT OF SHIT UPON MY SHOE

With disingenuous heart and yielding sigh
putting on long sleeves dutifully I
attend the funeral of old Doctor Clack
with all the locals in their suits of black
and you, in your expensive suit of blue,
with a bit of shit upon your shoe.

I catch your eye and point at
the brown distracting fecal splat.
With comprehending squint you lean my way
whisper, "I know," and go on to say,
"I put it there; there's a method to
having shit upon your shoe.

People like me, begrudge me not
my clothes, my house, expensive yacht,
prefer to hear of debt and not success,
for this they trust me none-the-less.
There is as simple reason I'll share with you:
it's because of this shit upon my shoe.

We're all insecure, you'll have to agree;
this shit makes people feel better than me.
They sense the advantage is always theirs,
and so I endure the sympathetic stares,
while getting the best of folks like you
who can't get past the shit on my shoe.

I treat everyone inordinately nice,
then I ask them for their sage advice.
question attentively in full detail
concerning those matters in which I fail.
So my good fortune, status too,
I owe it all to this shit on my shoe.

So there you have it in black and white.
I admit that I'm wrong while you are right,
send ingratiating notes for the least of deeds;
it's like I'm planting reciprocity seeds.
My formula for fruition, it's tried and it's true,
And it all starts with this shit upon my shoe."

WHAT FEELS GOOD IN THE HAND

The way an object fits into the hand
by design or nature
offers a reimbursement
of tactile satisfaction:

the ballast handle of a revolver, a bat,
the left hand's love affair with the
slender neck of a guitar and the right hand's
affinity for the coffee cup

few will argue the newly laid hen's egg
gratifies the palm, though this is not
the egg's purpose, as it is not the goal
of the river stone, a companion's
warm hand, or the baby's head nesting
in the cup of careful fingers.

What could be more luxurious
to a man's hand, be it callused or soft,
than the supple weight, the warm curvature
of a woman's breast?
Like sleep or prayer or tears of remorse,
it brings the angry dogs to heel.

WRONG WAY BUFFET

You are at the buffet
and of course you're famished
but the plates are small
more like saucers.

You try to moderate, but
the food presented is progressively
more appetizing until at the end
you come to the roast beef

and have to drape
your meat across a pile
that has become indistinguishable
as scalloped potatoes and fruit salad.

I'm that small plate at the buffet
learning to start with the roast beef
and apologizing my way against
the flow of procedural diners.

REGARDING EMILY DICKINSON

While walking through a day of spring
A pleading squall I heard,
Searched to find fallen from its nest
A helpless fledgling bird.

Small and flightless, a downy fluff,
It scuttled across the ground,
Calling predators to the feast
Bawling its pitiful sound.

Bending to cup it in my hands,
In doubt I then withdrew,
With virtue always a sacrifice
And this one nature's due.

The morning next I passed again
The place of my unrest,
To find the parents of that bird
Had returned it to the nest!

Is optimism a bitter hoax
Of our dream that good will reign?
Or do fools just never seek the truth,
Only deliverance from the pain?

THE VILLAGE IDIOT

She wore a plucking thimble on her thumb
and sitting on an apple box would hold
the headless pink birds by orange feet
over a fire to singe the pin feathers.

Chicken heads, eyelids down like window
Shades shut to the sun
Were scattered about where
She had axed them off.

Cohesive puddles of darkening blood,
Refused entry into the dusty earth,
Radiated out from the chopping block
Where bodies, free finally from the
Protestant temperance of chicken propriety,
Danced to outrageous rhythms and
Flapped frantically in the direction of
A small boy screaming away in panic,
Who much later would make the connection
Between this fiasco and dinner.

A small boy who ranged within what his
Mother thought was the safety of the farmyard,
Learning to throw and climb, of birth and death,
Seasons and Nature, gravity and inertia,

A small boy forgetting to hold on while
Exploring the upper reaches of the apple tree,
Falling, to be caught by the foot
In the crotch of a branch near to the ground.

His mother recovered him upside down
Saying if that tree hadn't been a mother herself,
And taken pity on his sorry circumstance,
He might have become the village idiot.

Now, I wonder, what would be so bad about that:
No expectations, an excuse to be eccentric,
Like Leroy Graham, whose mother's car hit a guard rail,
And who wandered our hometown behind a scarred forehead,
Perchance comprehending everything,
Appreciating the privileges, laughing back at the snickers,
wandering blamelessly into the girl's dressing room at the swimming pool.

MY MOTHER'S WORDS

'If you don't hoard and you care
someone else will have a share.'

Advice of a mother to her son
returning marbles I had won

In a game at school we had played.
'A friend you've kept is a friend you've made.'

'Resistance comes with a novel view
and critical words you'll come to rue.'

'When engaged in gossip,' her words I recall,
'If no good can be said, speak not at all.'

'With other's feeling your actions wed;
wear their shoes before you choose,' she said.

'Be unique in what you do
forbid others to prejudice you.'

The memories of my mother
have flown distant like winter birds,
but I mind and practice—like scripture—
the poetic wisdom of her words.

DIFFERENT AND THE SAME

My lungs yearn to breathe the air
of far places
rich with the particulate
of different cultures,
although it is the same air
I breathe here, gazing out
on the woods below my house.

My feet itch to walk along rivers
with different names
off different mountains on different continents
although it is the same water,
come back as snowflakes,
I tip my head back to and
let fall enticingly on my tongue
here in my backyard.

My ears lean away from here
for the song of foreign tongues,
their quick variable pitches,
yet they are expressing the same doubts
I hear in my hometown.

My eyes squint wistfully over horizons
to imagine the colors of women's dresses
and hues of the earth bathed in sunsets
at other latitudes,
although they are designed by the same artist
on the same canvas
that I will find wherever I am
if I allow my eyes to relax.

My nose is alert to unaccustomed scents
curry, eucalyptus, saffron and jacaranda,
portents of the exotic
that are no more rich and varied
than the familiar:
lilac, sage, fresh bread, good soil.

I must balance this fundamental hunger
For adventures I may never taste
With a greater appreciation of the usual
And a love of the common place.

CLEAN THE GLASS

Like the chorus of a ballad
The refrain of sleep comes round,
The part we all can sing together
A melody that's sunrise bound.

Light of morning, a whole new verse,
Words we've never heard will start,
Clouds or sunshine, day's delivery
Shines on windows of our heart.

The temper of the song depends on
How our windows refract the light.
Someday streams in, pure and golden,
Illuminating perspectives blithe.

Other mornings we wake to shadows
Singing sadly some requiem mass.
It's not the song or clouds that haunt us,
Just a need to clean the glass.

WE BEGIN EARLY

We begin early to shape ourselves
 to fit this world like a carver forms
a block of wood into Madonna.

We have little skill in this art,
but our strokes become finer
as we progress.

The block of wood we are given
Is a variable we cannot control.
If it is oak our development is

slow and arduous, if it is pine
our product takes early form,
appears polished.

Our wood may come with knots and
burls, hardened deformities we must
allow to exist in our sculpture.

These binds and the tight grain of hard
woods may leave us course and
complicated, appearing unfinished,

but with a strength to endure
the weathering of time, and
be improved in the bargain.

While the humble soft wood,
more easily formed and adapted,
will float high in the floods to come

and be assimilated in new
experiences as it is swept in
the direction of different.

SPRING JUST WENT PAST

And you were so preoccupied with your projects that Spring,
with its profanity of garrulous color and paint box of sweet
smells, passed right by you, unnoticed, until you found your coat
hanging in the garage, covering the calendar that was still on March.

It is because you are just a snowman inside one of those glass
balls full of liquid, waiting to be turned upside down, sending snowflakes
swirling, a snowman with eyes looking out but not seeing anything
but the snowstorm inside his little world. You vow that next year
you're going to set a lawn chair in the back yard and participate
in spring's eruption.

But next year you'll be looking out and not seeing past your own
snowstorm again, and spring, a fast paint horse approaching from the rear,
will romp past you so unexpectedly that by the time you get your head
out of your ass, all you'll see is a last glimpse of a colorful flank
disappearing into the verdant flush of summer.

PERSONIFICATION

The trill of a nesting Redwing
to my ear is happiness heard
'cause Momma always said to me,
'He's free as a bird.'

I believe Chickadee's character
is to sing the joyous part
cause Momma always said to me,
'She's happy as a lark'.

The Canyon Wren's cascading song
high upon the rocky wall,
Momma always said his song's so long
to hide the fact that he's small.

Killdeer's fluttering antics,
happy gambols without a toy,
Momma said she frolics so
because she's drunk with joy.

Blackbird, wren, killdeer, lark
demonstrate, prepared to die,
defend their chosen territory—oh
how mommas personify.

STREET LADY

Old, hunch-backed,
Elephant ankles swollen out of tired red slippers,
Scaly scalp in the April sunshine
shows through weedy hair.

Sitting talking to herself
on the steps of The Sharper Image
in San Francisco's Ghirardelli Square,
sipping port from a bottle
she keeps in her Nordstrom sack.

This contradiction requests I take a picture.
Who would notice,
so many tourists with cameras?

Then, something my mother said when I was ten,
staring at an Indian man come to town
in braids and blanket,

"Maybe you too can become a pebble,
with independent strength to stand
against the toneless stares of a monolith."

LIFE AIN'T MADE FOR LOOKING

Been on this train since the Spanish-American War.
Woke up in the seat I was sitting in when I went to sleep.
Fell asleep when I couldn't look at another Kansas
Cornfield. Woke up looking at a cornfield. Could have
Been Colorado, I don't know. But I do know
Life ain't made for lookin.'

Been on this train since Texas seceded from the union.
Feel like a Civil War veteran in the same underpants,
Looking out the same window at sunshine my
image would love to cast a shadow in, thinking
This life ain't made for lookin.'

Been on this train since the Dodgers left Ebbits Field.
Still sitting in the dugout being
A spectator, waiting to get in the game.
Life ain't made for lookin.'

Been on this train since I got on it and
I'll be on it till I get off. It's like a prison
Sentence being on this train, looking out
Barred windows wondering about life
On the outside and all that I'd do, thinking
Life just ain't made for lookin.'

EMPTY BUCKETS

It was the pleading, painful clang
That I first was made aware,
A sorry sour song sang
Of water that wasn't there

The smallest pebble of discontentment
Had fallen into my pail
Stamped epistle, unceremoniously sent
An overdue notice come by mail

My bucket was empty, dry as a bone
Not a drop was left to absorb the fall
Of slings to suffer and sudden stones
That are certain in life to call

Each must learn to keep their bucket full
The tenant verse of the poem 'To Be'
The soul self in the simple rule
Of responsibility

BUILDING A ROCK WALL

'Something there is that doesn't love a wall',
Robert Frost suggested, but me…
I love the idea of a rock wall,
how it promotes the history of the Earth
and allows me safely to pet a horse.

Walls of irony rummaging through our unpracticed vocabulary
adamantine, vehement, incontestable,
masculine in completion, feminine in creation;
felicitous, capricious, tactile.
More an act of discovery than creativity
this building of a rock wall.
No need for a blueprint, just fellowship
Of stone and skin.

A pile of rocks that hold hermaphroditic partnerships
waiting for affirmation
to be fit together like words in a relationship
determined by fate.

I let my eyes stumble over the chaos of basalt
in search of a corner that pleases, an interesting face,
and it emerges like the development of a sneeze;
progressively, a joining of forces,
and I am integrated into the rhythm of possibility,
in syncopation with this wall.
I fall under the influence of my own nature,
working with my hands and singing aloud,
transported under the authority of immediacy.

Unselfishly
the rocks volunteer themselves to this fusion
that I show to a passing neighbor.
He sees the wall, while I am enticed by the process,
the being present in the grace of confederations,
a euphony of words: falling in love,
the smell of passion fruit and coffee,
song of Jobim and meadowlarks.

FOR JUST SIXTY SECONDS

For just sixty seconds I'd like
to see the river without water
or interview my dog.

For just sixty seconds I'd like
to have my mother back,
to walk with her in silence.

For just sixty seconds I'd like
to see myself through my children's eyes,
understand calculus,
play the guitar perfectly,
see through cotton summer dresses,
dunk a basketball,
and purge all the hatred from the hearts of men.

For just sixty seconds I'd like
to address the sizeable crowd of those who have hurt me,
forgive them their insensitivities and announce
that the banquet lunch will be liver.

THE DARK CLOSET

FREEDOM FROM THE NEED TO KNOW

allows a woman to never have to look in the toilet
tank or consider her transmission's inner self.
There are guys for this, and guys are always available.

She doesn't need her flannel shirt unsnapped
two from the top or to have long voluptuous hair,
Men are hardwired for heroics, and the need
for men's heroics is at an all-time high.

They will work for an appreciative word, and
besides, women know from childhood they
lord over men's intellect. I mean, intuition
trumps intellect, right?

If a man senses he's being watched he's usually
wrong. But if he is right, it is because he's got
corn in his beard. Men need to know how things
work because their self-esteem depends on it.

What men don't know, even if they need to, is
how relationships work. Women understand how
relationships work and are frequently in their
relationship's toilet tank fixing things.

Here's the deal. Women and men are different sub-species,
who, like the coyote and the poodle, are just barely close enough
genetically to interbreed. And, as it is for the coyote and the poodle,
this is an awkward thing for men and women, all driven by something

neither of them understand, coming together in confusion, and
producing feral, curly-coiffured hybrids who go off
wild-eyed and unprepared on
a road of self destruction.

GAMBLERS

At the table sat five gamblers
love and luck were two
a third was fate, the other hate
the last chair left for you.

After the shuffle the deck was cut
and the cards were passed about
bets were made as the hands were laid
and the only voice was doubt.

The silence gathered and settled there;
five hands were quiet too.
All eyes ascended and lit intended
upon the loser...you.

HOW GOD SCREWED UP

Dog can support so many fleas,
then the dog dies and the fleas
are shit out of luck.

I'm talking about the Earth, and
you, and how it came to be that
the Earth has so many fleas.

Let's blame this problem on God.
God's a single guy, right?
His only begotten son was born

by immaculate conception.
This is because the idea of sex
gives God the creeps.

So when God said, "Go forth
and be fruitful, overrun
the Earth with yourself,"

he was afraid his original plan
of babies by sex, would be too
disgusting. Something

had to be done about the
creepiness of sex or fruitfulness
would be out of the question.

So he went to the lab and
came up with this sticky stuff
called testosterone, which,

like Round Up-ready corn
and fast food, created more
problems than it solved.

Testosterone made hair
grow in funny places. It
made muscles get big

instead of brains. But mostly
it made sex, which still gives
God the creepy shivers, wildly fun.

So fruitful went viral,
and God's little lap dog
The Earth is now crawling

With fleas that are about to
kill it. And it's God's fault for
dickin' around with something
he didn't understand.

NOW THAT I AM DEAD

There's no longer any purpose to put on the happy face
that I wore through life, or to make the most of things,
as was the counsel of my father, or more annoying still,
to find something nice to say, my mother's daily caveat.

With these put-on qualities taken off, along with these
ridiculous clothes I was expected to wear, I am free to
express a few posthumous resentments,
like the Star Spangled Banner before every game
and monogamy. I think I speak for all guys
when I wonder, 'Isn't monogamy a hard wood?'

Fear of authority always bugged me, spinster teachers
with rulers and smug little cops with dark glasses too big
for their heads. The guilt we were all baptized in is a big resentment
of mine, like some device they implanted in us as babies, releasing
small quantities of anguish when we forgot our mother's
birthday, lied in confession, or left the toilet seat up.

And now that I am dead and don't care what you think,
I would like to add: I prefer the company of whores
and alcoholics to anybody associated with organized
religion or you.

FENDER SKIRT

I like fender skirt.
I think it is pleasant the way
it rolls on my tongue when
I say it: fender skirt.

I have never especially cared
for the look of fender skirts,
making a car look disproportionately
heavy and low in the rear.

I think of a pear or a bowling pin
or that woman who works at
the post office near my home,
who, like a '57 Ford, has an

appealing grille, lithe lines
of hood and windshield, carrying
my eyes to a ponderous fender-
skirted rear end.

Fender skirt, fender skirt, fender skirt.

WHACKIN' THE SACK

"Someone has to do it."
This is Pierre, the handyman,
whose job it is to see to it
the feral cat population
doesn't get too troublesome.

So often, certainly beyond expected
proclivity, these cats reproduce
like rabbits, and, with so many
porous outbuildings on the farm,
Pierre made the rounds daily,

looking for hidden litters. Then
into the sack they'd go, no
ceremony or sorrow, just a
sturdy stick, and you'd hear Pierre
out there whackin' the sack.

WORRY

Worry like nice tits
on a tense woman
is busy in your head
while leaving your hands idle

It won't matter one whit
what it is you're doing
peeling potatoes or
walking along the creek

Those tits will show up
and incarcerate your thoughts until
you are so frantic to deal with them
you do something irrational

Like making overtures of commitment
that are ridiculously insincere
and if you're lucky you get those tits
out of your head and into your hands

And only then do you realize
what an obsessed son of a bitch you are
to have spent all that time on what?
But the phone interrupts your self-derision;
it is the woman
calling in a few promises,
and now you really have
something to worry about.

I CAN'T NOT LOVE THIS WORLD

I'm sick and I love the memory of health.
I'm feeling good and I love feeling good.
At night I love the adventure of sleep.
In the morning I love the light revealing the world again.
I love the idea of recovery from disappointment.
I love caring. I especially love not caring.
I love trees more than people, but not more
than my wife. I love life, every maintenance-required,
Dying, putrefying, unfair-fucking bit of it.
I love that it is always there--the moment.

Thanks

To my friends and family, who don't laugh and point any longer. Now they just laugh and pat me consolingly on the back.

To my friend Kay Landis for editorial support and to her friend David Freeman for graphic support.

To my wife Martha, for a lot of stuff. Like my beautiful children and her killer tuna casserole.

www.ingramcontent.com/pod-product-compliance
Lightning Source LLC
Chambersburg PA
CBHW031427290426
44110CB00011B/561